Winter Solstice and What Follows

By

Ryan Fredric Steinbeck

Winter Solstice and What Follows

Ryan Fredric Steinbeck

ISBN: 978-0-578-15407-7

Photographs by Cynthia Steinbeck
Cover design by Michael R. Steinbeck

First Printing

Acknowledgements:

I'm indebted to my wife Cindy for the photos, the advice and criticism on many of these poems, and for her continual display of unrelenting excitement toward the holiday season.

Thanks to Michael Steinbeck for the illustration and covers, and the patience with me this year.

Thanks to my family and friends for support.
Thanks to Abby Collins and Myles Evans.
Thanks to my school band teacher, the late Lance Haas, the reason I started analyzing music which led to the writing of my first poems.
Thanks to all artists that are inspired and, as a result, continue to inspire.

To The Reader

Over the past year I started setting
aside winter and Christmas themed
poems that didn't "fit" into previous
collections. It wasn't until I
realized how enjoyable it was to write
for this season that I started working
on poems specifically for this
collection. So here we are.
Thank you for your support. Here's to
eternally happy winters and
Christmases full of family gatherings,
love, and laughter.

Ryan Steinbeck

"What good is the warmth of summer, without the cold of winter to give it sweetness?"
– **John Steinbeck,**

Contents:

Contents:

A Winter Tale Parts I-IV

Winter Solstice

At some mysterious point in time
The shortest day and the longest night
where autumn leaves turn to the first snow

Rising light illuminates the passage
The chamber fills with a golden warmth

A flat surface toward the setting winter sun
The Altar stone and Slaughter stone align

A circle where the sun rises and sets
through openings to the southeast to southwest

Stonehenge, Newgrange, and Gosek circle
welcome the winter solstice

Born of Neolithic times
Traditions bursting with tales
Crops sewn and harvested
in harmony with nature
to behold and observe this mastery

Impatience to patience
Hysteria to calm
Rain to snow
Something in the solar system shifts
a turning page
to the year's final chapter
How can we not commemorate or celebrate?

Snowbird

Blue grey contrast
Waiting his turn to feed
Back and forth
from the crimson branch
to the bare shrub
He slaps his wings against his breast
scattering the snow
stealing sounds away
from the morning buzz
from other feathery songs
But he has every right
He has found his place here
among the others
in this uniform carousel
His way is majestic, secret
well known to us

Stark
Wind-harrowed
Intractable
He stays
Everyday
He spreads his little sliver of cheer
without ever being aware

Snowfall In Sunlight

A withered sapling
Flood of white
Downtime for spring
for it to be replaced
for winter to give its worth
Condensation on glass
A prism of light
A greyness of sky
The last leaf on a tree
hangs on for dear life
aware of its fate
Sooner or later the time arrives

Life is not part of us
We are part of life
We look beyond designations
to spread ancient cheer and wisdom
or we could pause for a moment
turn off our minds
as we turn off the lights
appreciate the infrequency of the moment
the reasons painters exist
Snowfall in sunlight

Wake Up

On this cold winter day
peel back the layers
let the warmth underneath escape
Remember the banks of the river
where we left it all
where there is now snow fall

This is more
A different conversation
on a similar platform
in the trance of a morning haze
awareness spills over like snow melt
For a scarce additional moment
it accepts your offer to be still

Your dreams bloom in high altitudes
Snow falls as light as petals
on tired wilting leaves
like the view from your snow globe

Thought eventually finds you
amidst your morning state
emancipated from your restraint
It disturbs your rapid eye movement
The beginning of your new day
Welcome back

Spirit

At November's end
She sets the clock back
She sets herself back to eight years old
Her eyes innocent and wide
Her spirit invincible
as she turns over the Christmas leaf

She believes in Santa Claus
Reindeer on rooftops
Snowmen that come to life

A year can grow tiresome
Daily life can cloud her vision
For her the smile returns
Simply in slumber
was the spirit I feared broken

She never needs a reason to give
In her fashion she celebrates and sings
in one hundred beautiful ways

I'd have to be in a comatose state
to be unaffected
by the way she's affected
by her unyielding spirit

The Winter Squirrel

In large numbers
we take to the streets
going about habitual routines
Trees are transportation systems
With every leap I fly close to the end

Now it's here again
I've been preparing for months
for this time of year
And then came you
Red, young, and indigent
Tagging along to the feeders
Following me to the tree tops
Begging for portions
of my home, my food
You are nuts to think
I'd be willing
to give you the nuts I keep

Where did you come from?
Why are you still around?
I'll have you know
I'm a cold winter squirrel
set in my ways
and you're gnawing on my nerves
wedging into my colony

But the snow falls in peace
and this Christmas thing is near
I realize
I'm used to being annoyed by you
How else would I occupy my time?
I set aside my rations
expand my fortress in the trees
Christmas time is for things like this
so I'm told
I suppose there's room for one more

The *No Santa* Clause

Harbored in a featureless, barren world
A strange force emerges
with a rickety old sled
and a couple of reindeers
attending flight school

He's the Archbishop of the South Pole
up for the challenge
of dethroning the man in the North Pole
Everyone benefits from competition

He knits a suit in blue, not red
He builds a castle to store his merchandise
He bought in bulk and needs to advertise
find some elves willing to switch sides
and change the minds of the entire planet

Instead of kids he'll call them clients
He'll have them sign a contract
In fine print a *No Santa Clause*
naming him their exclusive supplier
He'll make everyone so happy they'll forget
about their jolly washed up hero

His first marketing trip
Children cried, parents called him creepy
He fails and fails again
Months go by, a letter received
A north pole return address
From Santa it read
Welcome to the fold
It's great to have a friendly rivalry
to keep me on my toes
We should meet for lunch half way
wherever that may be
P.S- You need a kid friendly name

7

The archbishop scratched his head
He expected war and received peace
He assessed his ill begotten gains
The convoluted whisper of the half man
and half angry child that remains

The adornment of drama and conflict
A driving force behind his existence
Without it there's no fire remaining
He opens the phone book
of characters believed to be fictional
Maybe Santa has an open position
If he can't beat them
He'd might as well join them

Winter Waltz

With cane in hand
I limp toward center stage
To a chorus of groans and boos
you always know I'm coming
You're never ready

I ease in unnoticed
Then thrash and twist, bellow and howl
To you I warm up
then turn a cold shoulder
You may think this is a devils deal
As I slap you
in your figurative collective faces

An onus that owns up to my mythology
This time you won't have the foggiest
what I have in store
It will be bigger, better than the rest
You'll wish you never wished for this
You'll never want to see me again

But oh how the memory fades
You always want what isn't there
I'll waltz to the side where I'll stay
until it's my turn to cut in again
after you've had enough
of those other seasons

Off The Market

Influenced by the dense winter air
For one night we give it our all
Shedding our unsociable skin
Wearing our best sewn and painted faces

Displays in the windows
I'm last year's holiday bargain
My seams don't line up
The sale doesn't catch any eyes
except one
I've never felt more profitable

The face of a stranger
Her expression clear through fogged glass
and developing snow
A look of intent
suggesting more than courtesy
Perhaps it's my smile catching your eye
or my aftermarket price

We exit to the street
The surge in my veins
A rush of confidence
born from the thrill
To share a moment like this
To know you exist
That you're permanently
willingly
happily
unequivocally
off the market

It Stays

Innocence of moments
Joy of the season
The peace inside
That spends the entire year arriving

The gatherings
Heart felt wishes
Warm scarves and coats
Flickering lights
Pureness of hearts in contiguity

Departure is inevitable
It comes back around
to the certainty of the season
the joy of all smiles
the urgency to love now
Carry it to the end of days
The belief in all good things
It stays

Steam Powered Engine

Water removed from mines
for these external combustion engines
This Rankine cycle
spurred the industrial revolution

I've dreamt this one thousand times
Never have I questioned
Tonight I watch steam in the cold air
as it makes demands
as large clouds dissipate
Ice crystals form and gather
atop the steel chimney

On through Netherton
We are headed anywhere
with no determined return

Old windows let in the cold
We huddle up for the long haul
An ungrateful soul may be discouraged
We're pleased to have been given time
and the resources to get away

Good will is reciprocating
Optimism the dominate source
retrofitting the journey
with the destination
Steam powered engine
we're relying on you
to get us there and take us home

For These Times

We allow the year to run rampant
It's built in our code
except for one loop hole

As the final segment crests before us
We hope to condense the expanded
come back to what matters most

If these final hours mean anything
let's set aside our differences
return to what we know

Our futures are silenced
by the weight of our choices
In a circle of wind
There are those for whom you'd do anything
Who'd do anything for you

The lucky and fortunate
will be close enough to embrace
If this day was everyday
perhaps we'd lay down the weapons
leave the foreign lands
Love could fill the empty cracks
as we watch the world go by

I will truly listen
I will be all that you imagine
Made whole by the presence and energy
of fellow life travelers
There is nowhere else I'm supposed to be
I'm so thankful for these times

Wheel House

Her coat isn't warm enough
She's fine with that
Frost on the wheel house
It's dark when she transforms
The time is near and far
She escapes by remaining
The snow, light
The season is approaching

Memories are the footings
She builds
Just as yesterday
today will be remembered
She's here for the view
Not before do the holidays seem real
Tomorrow is anxiously beckoning
The snow, heavy
The season is here

Follow the Star

A father said to his son
Find a reason to be whole
a cause to carry you
a means of staying honest and true
before the eyes of others
and in the quiet time of exclusion

Find the star that guides you
That gives you the sense of direction
You may find your star in the desert
on a beautiful, cold winter's night
or over the Arabian sea
You may find it on the tip of a pen
or in the beauty of trees
In the strumming of strings
or in chorus and verse
If you find your star and follow it
until the last of your days end
you will defy all constraints upon you
and you will be free

A Childs Hand

Electric with innocence and wonder
he needs me to tell him
there are fields of snow
before there are fields of snow
He needs my reassurances
When I don't follow through
he remembers

I could be the stem of the plant
that becomes the curing tree
or dries and fades
with crumbled leaves

I am a pinnacle
the reason he believes
I tip toe through my vocabulary
I navigate and temper my display
knowing he'll buy into truths
but also into delusions
It will shape parts of his soul
I may never see

I could be the light that carries him
from which he draws in critical times
or the dark gaping hole
he'll never be able to explain
what's missing and why

Before I take the child's hand
do I understand
the weight of this journey?
Am I ready to be nothing?
Am I ready to be everything he needs?

Whispering Pines

Today my arms are open wide
listening to the whispering pines
Branches bow to the rustle
Remnants of high fresh snow above
fall to us after the sway
onto the ground, our heads and arms

It's a sign of an older time
we carry with us through the night
Our thoughts a snow drift in the wind
where ideas of goodwill begin

They watch us from the window
We decorate for all to see
A change in heart inevitable
If I plunge into the season's essence
If I'm plagued by your passion

Everything I love is here
under the whispering snowy pines
that grew and settled long ago
within this peaceful time
If they are still here and alive
I know there is a reason
They see everything and still rise
Who am I to question?

We rejoin the anxious hearts inside
The day they wait for is after this night
We set aside petty thoughts and crimes
to exist within the moment
block out the days ahead and behind
All is forgiven on this winter's eve
Smiles are the same down the line
It's alright to feel this way tonight
Maybe for the rest of my time
Everything I love is here

To Say

On the day before the new day
my heart is uncaged
You are the fog over the cold
lifting

I allowed you to suffer
in the here and here after
Your image in the sun
will reach me always
Your voice in the wind chills me

So I am the late fall tree
dropping leaves
I let go

It was never my intention
to hold on to you this long
to muddle the passage of your true way
but the last goodbye
is the most difficult to say

Christmas Nog

Someone should've cut me off the nog
three glasses ago
I think I have my wits about me
as I slur my words
and turn into a feature presentation
But it's Christmas wine
at Christmas time

The next morning my face in the mirror
Spectacles and a beard drawn in marker
Everyone appeared surprised
Nobody willing to fess up
except for a good laugh at my expense

At home on Christmas morning
Presents beneath the tree
Santa had come and gone

I unwrapped an unmarked DVD and pushed play
I had been passed out on the couch
when a reindeer licked my face
It was Santa with the marker
He left a note inside the case
Sorry son, I couldn't resist
just having some fun
Please don't show this to anyone
Because you know I'll know if you do
and yes, if you hadn't guessed by now
I exist and what they say about me is true

My Only True Christmas Gift

There's room for the clouds
where our wings collide
within the invasive jet stream
She shades a glance in my longitude
I was a phrase in a lost sentence
She was unfazed by me
She had her winter remembrances
She long embraced her traditions
I won't be her revelation
She doesn't need or want me to be
She pulls apart the evergreens
analyses her layers
She can give herself
and remain who she is
She is my only true Christmas gift

Christmas Morning

My eyes open
after enduring the eve with relatives
after a lot of stirring and little sleep
after listening for footsteps on the roof
and wondering if he came down the chimney
and if he liked his cookies

I rise and tap on my brother's door
We tiptoe down the stairs
He was here, the cookies are gone
He left icy footprints on the carpet
How did they remain so long?

Presents a mile high
We're only allowed to divide them
and empty our stockings
For a seeming eternity we are just kids
until we hear weight shifting
and movement from the floor above
voices and creaking stairs

Christmas morning, our favorite morning
is officially about to begin

Stuck In Traffic On Christmas Day

Packed like lemmings into shiny metal
boxes
Says the angelic voice on the radio
I can't think of a more applicable phrase
Nothing original that's better
These words are a clean fitted suit
worn for this precise situation
I said I would be there hours ago
They demanded it be yesterday

I wear my good thoughts like a ski mask
covering my irate curse words
I'm not patient
I just hide my impatience well
My insistence is a needle on my skin
deeper with every delay

Idling across from a small town center
Buildings are immersed in decorations
Their Christmas tree touches the sky
A snowball fight breaks out
between children and adults
as a boy diverts from the cross fire
and tackles a large Santa decoration

I all but abandon my anger
as a smile sneaks onto my face
This season turns over stones
and new leaves
with the wealth of emotions it can sway
A heart that forgets remembers to believe
Even though I'm stuck in traffic
on Christmas day

In Solitude The Snowfall
-A Winter Tale Part I

Long ago
When autumn lost to winter
The ending of days
was the beginning day

In solitude the snow falls
Beautiful and bittersweet
Disintegrating and restorative
Wind and deafening silence
barricades the cabin
I am a boy lost in the woods

As I turn toward pale light
The mirror inside my soul
reflects the anxious turnings
I stand among fallen leaves
The year has taken its toll

Thankful for numb fingers
cold responses and harsh settings
a stirring warmth of smiles
thawed hearts and hot tea
when the winter snow turned welcoming

Moonlight scurries behind tree tops
The dark, cold woods
turn vibrant again in daylight
The warm fire before me
I am rejuvenated and humbled
I see where I could've been more for you
understanding why I'm alone
For now it's a welcoming reflection
I consider going home for the holidays

Eyes of Fire
-A Winter Tale Part II

These woods have been good to me
Such calm
Wildlife feeds from my hand
I needed this time here
but the winters have become lonely

There's a settlement two miles away
I frequent the market on the corner
I thought about her before we met
Then here she is in real time
as my disregarded dreams described her
deciding between flowers I don't recognize

I was a man of stone as she approached me
In an instance my soul is decorated
by the lights and tinsel of her smile
It was as if there was dialogue before
Joining a regularly scheduled program
already in progress

I could feel her river underneath
gushing with icy anticipation
I found passage at ground level
I kneeled at her shore
I hadn't realized how much hope I'd lost

I returned to my cabin that evening
In a letter I apologized to family
I explained to them my estrangement
and that coming home may not be of fables

I turn to her eyes of fire
in the wide open winter skies
I feel an unexpected warmth
How quickly hope can return

A Prepared Meal
-A Winter Tale Part III

The space rented in my head
Now up for lease
My long term isolation will end
The lights here will go out
I've spent my last holiday alone

I befriend the day
preparing my favorite meal
I am determined and vigilant
as one by one
I set the dishes in the rotunda
on the edge of the property
where the animals come to feed
It is my thank you and farewell
You've helped me more than I can say

I spend the evening packing
then the most peaceful night of sleep
On my front steps in the morning
Seeds, nuts, and vegetables
scattered in uniformity
It's wonderful to know the feelings mutual

I am in the open
I look to the woods
They are with me in white paintings
We are prisoners in the present
The observers are soldiers of silence
Eyes of sorrow looking back
I say this is not good bye forever
I know they hear me
I know they understand
as they fade into the snowy background

The Arrival
-A Winter Tale Part IV

I park the car at the local diner
It looks to have changed hands again
I'm across from the fire station
in the unincorporated outskirts
I walk the empty, slippery streets
Guidance from infrequent lamp posts
Orange lights are mini beacons
on every other corner

Snow begins to fall
lightly at first, then increases
I climb the crest of the hill
Where I would play as a child
The town lights paint the horizon
The town tree is smaller than I remember

We agreed I would venture here alone
tell them of her and our plans
Like the pace of last minute shoppers
My heart rate surges as I approach
Blood rushes, thoughts are racing
I arrive at the familiar poorly lit plot
set apart from the newer developments
Little has changed in my time away
I reach the familiar gate
walk to the familiar side door

After ten long years
I wonder if this is the right thing to do
I answer my own question
I know it is
I wrap on the old wooden door
I hear voices and patters of footsteps
Decibels rise acknowledging an arrival
In a moment the season's true meaning
will arrive in my heart

Kringle's Farewell

I have to be the oldest man alive
but I love my job and have no intent to rest
The build and crescendo to frenzy
A yearlong anticipation

What most consider freezing to me is tropical
Still I enjoy getting out from time to time
Every city, state, province, and country
I stop the world to accomplish it all

Though I admit the travel takes its toll
By the end of my flight I live a year in a day
I feel I need to get away, dream it up again
Maybe die my hair
shave my beard
blend in with the crowd
hit a country bar or a rave
drink coffee in the tropics midday
read of romances in a Paris hotel
go spelunking into the depths of the earth
then hibernate and hide way

Like a phoenix I will burn to ash
Rising again as does the sun
ideally with new methods and ideas
Different ways to contemplate
Different things to say
Different means to say them
I will be renewed, revised, reinvented
Ready to begin again

See you next year

Notes on the Poems

Winter Solstice and What follows:

New Grange is an ancient temple over 5,000 years old along the River Boyne in Ireland. It points to the winter solstice sunrise, which provides illumination of its passage and chamber through a roof-box above the entrance. It allows sunlight to fill the chamber during the winter solstice period.

From early morning, December 19th to 23rd, a fine beam of light penetrates the roof-box and graces the chamber floor where it ultimately reaches the rear of the chamber. The beam widens as the sun rises and eventually the entire room is illuminated for approximately 17 minutes.

Stonehenge, near Wiltshire, England was constructed around the seventeenth century and is believed to be aligned on a sight-line that points to the winter solstice sunset.

Goseck circle, often called the German Stonehenge, is believed to be one of the oldest solar observatories. It's aligned to both the winter solstice sunset and sunrise

The *No Santa* Clause:

I doubt that the Archbishop is real. It's silly to make up fictional Christmas characters. There's only one real Santa Claus. But I gave my best shot.

The Winter Squirrel:

Squirrels can talk and deliberate, and they know what Christmas is. These are known facts.

Off The Market:
Excitement goes both ways. What thrills a toy must feel about being purchased

Steam Powered Engine:
My tribute to *The Polar Express*

Stuck In Traffic On Christmas Day:
The first line, *Packed like lemmings into shiny metal boxes,* is taken from the Police song *Synchronicity II* from the album *Synchronicity.* I felt like it embodied the feeling of the character at that moment in time.

www.ingramcontent.com/pod-product-compliance
Lightning Source LLC
Chambersburg PA
CBHW020445030426
42337CB00014B/1398